THE HEALING POWER OF BALANCED EMOTIONS

by DR. FREDERICK BAILES

A Series of Sunday Lectures
by FREDERICK BAILES
delivered at the
Fox-Wilshire Theatre
Los Angeles, California

DEVORSS *Publications*

ISBN: 0-87516-124-3

DeVorss & Company, Publisher
P.O. Box 550
Marina del Rey, CA 90294

Printed in the United States of America

CONTENTS

INTRODUCTION

ANY perfectly balanced machine runs more smoothly, uses less energy, and lasts longer than one which is out of balance. Man's body is a machine, subject to the same principle. It wears out rapidly under friction, developing weaknesses which it would avoid if it were brought under the control of balanced emotions.

This book is written for one purpose only. It is intended to point out those elements that make up the balanced personality, to the end that the individual shall enjoy harmonious relations with others and with himself. This balanced harmony possesses tremendous healing power, for it is akin to the fundamental hidden harmony of the universe, and of the unseen Intelligence which evidently lies behind all that is seen.

The healing of the body is not necessarily a religious process. True, many healings have occurred at religious shrines and under the impact of strong religious fervor. Such healings were not produced by adherence to any specific theological tenet, but by the re-balancing of the inner emotional and spiritual life of the subject. Thus, freed from the cross-pull of guilt, fear, hate, and resentment, his thought life has been brought into conformity with that Universal Intelligence, of which it has been said, "God is LOVE." This vast Love, or good will, then asserts its balanced harmony in him, as a river absorbs and calms the tumbling brook which has united with it.

Thus, healing is the result of a dual action. Man acts to re-establish his inner harmony. This places him in a mental and emotional position where something larger, deeper, and more permanent can move into action, reproducing within him that which is forever in balance, thereby healing the illnesses caused by the friction of his former imbalance. I have seen this occur so often that I am convinced that there is a very definite Law of Healing. Anyone can use it.

Chapter I

THE HEALING POWER OF OPTIMISM

DURING the past year, I have read about twenty books on the subject of optimism. I have been disappointed. They stress the importance of "going through life with a smile"; yet they furnish no clues to the inward peace and courage which would cause one to carry a smile. They seem rather to suggest a combination of will power and self-hypnosis by which one may habitually carry a "hail fellow well met" expression. Unsupported by any true philosophy of life, this can not properly be called optimism.

True optimism is a feeling of the expectancy of the good, based upon rational, logical grounds. It is a state of mind not worked up from the outside; it is rather the outgrowth of a continuing state of mind built up within the individual and resting on solid ground. It is optimism, for instance, to decide for oneself that life is not foe but friend, and that we do not require a ready-made condition of life in order to achieve happiness.

Helen Keller's book *Optimism* is a good treatment of the subject. While an infant, she became totally deaf and blind following an illness; she was dumb as a result. Having no means for communication with others, she was first taught to read by having her hand gently tapped.

Miss Keller's amazing development from deaf-mute baby to thoroughly expressive adult is self-evident in her book, written when she was twenty-three and a senior in college. In this volume, she lays the foundation for those attitudes which aggregate in optimism. She observed that nothing great was ever accomplished in a spirit of pessimism, because the pessimist has already concluded that there is nothing much that he can do to change disagreeable conditions. Miss Keller's own achievements stand as a grand example of the power of true optimism to take life by the throat.

OPTIMISM ACHIEVES

"No pessimist ever discovered a new star, or laid the foundation for an enduring organization." None ever penetrated the secrets of life, or explored a new country. The pessimist lacks that spark which by-passes the old and delves into the new and wonderful. The optimist is a person on the move, inspired by a feeling of expectancy; he knows that life does not have to be ready-made for him. No matter what others may think of life, he knows that the "I" in him can make life to its order; therefore he says, "*I* lay aside those things that would hem me in. *I* burst the barriers of fear or indolence. *I* reach out, pressing forward toward the mark of some high calling that beckons me on."

Miss Keller stresses the fact that optimism comes from believing, attempting, and achieving. Optimism of the right kind is always practical, because it emerges in constructive action. It might not always be successful, but this is not important. The important thing is that we start, try, dare, expend effort. The law of averages promises fair success, and this attitude of resourceful daring almost guarantees fulfillment.

The poet Byron rose above the ugliness of his clubfoot. He reached out and wrote some of the most beautiful verse in the English language.

Robert Louis Stevenson fought a lifelong battle with illness and became a literary giant. In spite of physical weariness and suffering, he wrote with bounce in his soul, as if he had reached outside himself and drawn in brightness, pleasure, gaiety, and joy in things he saw. His feeling was genuine, for he communicates it in every line, and the reader catches it.

Beethoven, deaf, ugly, living in a garret, reached

out far beyond his depressing surroundings and worked out those beautiful compositions that lift and steady men in all generations. He transcended adversity and brought beauty out of ugliness.

These men did not demand that life carry them on a pillow. They stood on their own two feet, legs apart, and dared life to come on. As someone has said, life does not consist in being dealt a good hand of cards, but in playing a poor hand well. This attitude is the true basis for that sort of optimism that raises the individual to the heights.

The story is told of a young doctor, called in to deliver a baby into a poverty-stricken family. The child had one cruelly deformed leg, and was having great difficulty breathing. He thought, "Why should I let him live? Poverty-stricken, crippled, called Limpy by others, he'll never be worth anything to himself or the world. I'll just do nothing for that breathing. It is better that he die."

Then he remembered his Hippocratic oath; he simply had to save that baby. He began blowing into its mouth until the lungs were acting normally and the child gave its first cry.

Years later, the doctor's daughter and her husband were killed in an auto accident. The doctor took their ten-year-old daughter to rear. One day a mysterious malady struck the child. It looked like polio; the best clinics determined that it was not polio, but a similar and incurable condition. The girl would be helpless for life.

He learned that there was a young doctor in a small town in the Middle West who had been getting excellent results in the treatment of this particular disease. They went west, the treatment was successful, and the little girl was returned to normal health.

This young doctor was lame. Comparing notes, they found that he was the deformed baby into whose mouth the doctor had breathed thirty years before. He had specialized in this crippling disease because of his own infirmity.

Pessimism would have left that deformed child to die. Optimism was the attitude which swept the feeling of hopelessness aside and determined to try to save the life. Optimism emerged in constructive action, which set in motion a chain of causation which magnified itself in the lives of many others as the years passed, and which ultimately circled back bringing its supreme good to the now old doctor.

The pessimist wishes for something, then immediately begins to think of all the reasons why it can not be brought to pass. The optimist delves beneath the discouraging surface, searches for all the reasons why the thing he wants can come true. Whether in health, finances, or any other discouragement, the answer comes in "can's" rather than "can't's."

"MIRACLES"

This brings us to the subject of "miracles," because many inexplicable spiritual healings are called "miracles" by those who do not understand. Many persons firmly declare that they do not believe in miracles. Neither do we, because we do not believe that spiritual healings are any contravention of natural and spiritual law. They are the result of the application of higher laws than those used in the laboratory.

Scientifically trained people sometimes assert that they do not believe in healings by prayer, miracles, or anything that contravenes natural law.

To which we would reply by asking, "Does any living man know *all* natural law? Is anyone sure that man has reached the limit of human knowledge, and that there are no more laws to be discovered? Has material science not confined its investigations exclusively to physical law, and shied away from anything that savored of the spiritual? Who then is competent to say that anything contravenes universal law? Or who has said the last word concerning material and physical law?"

We know today of many physical laws that were unknown hundreds of years ago, or even fifty years ago. Today we are using many natural laws that were unguessed at by our ancestors. And it is quite likely that our descendants will be using natural laws of which we are now in total ignorance. Our scientific knowledge is the best that has ever been, but it is by no means final. How then can anyone be so presumptuous as to say that *anything* violates natural law, when we admit that our knowledge of the forces operating in the universe is so incomplete?

The limit of possibility is constantly being raised by the discovery of additional facts. The writer of a recent scientific article brought out a most interesting fact. If the angle of the axis upon which the earth revolves would change to a very slight degree, things that appear miraculous would happen on earth. At the equator a man loses 1/289th of his weight because he is the farthest distant from the poles, the centers of rotation. So if it were possible for man somehow to speed up the earth's rotation in space by seventeen times, he would then weigh nothing at the equator, and with the proper adjustments he could float in space. If this increase in the earth's rotational speed occurred, the action of the natural laws would be quite different, but they would still be natural laws.

Moreover, although man's floating in space above the equator would then be considered miraculous, it could not properly be called a miracle; therefore, "miracles" are only the operation of laws of physics as yet undiscovered. Perhaps the metaphysics of today will be the commonly accepted physics of a later generation.

If someone had said one hundred years ago that we would travel from New York to London in a few hours, he would have been told that this would be a contravention of natural law. Since then, man has learned to use natural law to do this very thing. If someone had told one of the Pilgrim Fathers that one day a speech in London would be heard simultaneously in Boston, he would have been told that this was contrary to nature. Yet it was the optimistic approach to nature's own laws that gave us radio, television, and communication satellites.

LAWS UPON LAWS

Man's study of the universe is revealing that there are laws upon laws, and laws within laws. Beyond and behind the physical principles which have given man all his inventions lies a great realm of spiritual law "in which we live and move and have our being." Man has been so busy making himself a more comfortable animal that he has neglected a systematic study of these spiritual laws. Only recently has any serious effort been made to understand them. Yet they are closest to us, operate constantly within us, and are most vital to our happiness and well-being.

Life is like a jigsaw puzzle, and man is slow in getting all the pieces into place. He has found small fragments of law in the field of spiritual healing. These seem not to be tied to the physical at any point, and operate quite independently of the physical; yet they seem to make sense, for they result in the healing of seemingly incurable illnesses. Those who come later will build upon the work of the pioneers; they will fill in the intervening spaces, complete the jigsaw puzzle, and make a coherent whole. It will be known of a certainty that the spiritual healing principle is as valid as the first and second laws of thermodynamics, which operated in the universe for aeons before man discovered them.

Modern doctors have learned how to push the body temperature right up to the "burning up" limit, through fever therapy, with beneficial results to the patient. Why could it not be that under spiritual conditions a similar beneficial effect could be obtained through spiritual therapy? For every condition cured by fever therapy has been healed through optimistic prayer and spiritual treatment.

It could happen that some scientist of the future could learn how safely to speed up the action of a particular endocrine gland so that it would correct morbid conditions in every part of the body.

If this were to become standard medical practice in the future, why can it not be that the Infinite Healing Presence could produce today that certain healing substance unguessed at by present-day scientists with their incomplete knowledge? The Creator built the glands in the first place, manufactures the hormones in them momentarily, and knows all the laws before they are discovered. Whenever we are dealing with life, we are working with Infinite life as well as that of the individual; every cell that lives was built by the Intelligence with which we deal in spiritual healing.

Infinite Life beckons us on, and rewards us when we follow in its footsteps. Where Infinite law is observed, results follow. The true optimist is he who firmly believes that there are far higher powers operating in the healing of the body, and who dares to act as though this is true. In spite of the kindergarten state of our knowledge, it is remarkable how the spiritual laws of healing are producing results. The spiritual healer is an optimist.

THE INFINITE HEALING PRESENCE

What are these currents of life that move in and through the individual? They are difficult of definition or delineation. The best term is perhaps "The Infinite Healing Presence." For some that sounds theological; to us it seems rational and all inclusive.

What is the Intelligence that leads the bee and the ant to store up food for the winter when it has not yet experienced a winter in its short lifetime? What leads the stag beetle to drill a hole in the bark of a tree where it will stay, awaiting its metamorphosis into another form? And by what prescience does the male drill a hole twice as large as the female? How does he know that he will require extra room for the two staglike horns which will grow on his head? Some Intelligence higher than his own is operating within him.

The same Intelligence operates in the eel. Dr. Cressy Morrison, in *Man Does Not Stand Alone*, tells how every eel in the world comes to a spot in the Atlantic near Bermuda to spawn. From the Baltic, from Canada, from the Pacific Islands, from every river in the world, they converge annually on this particular spot. In those which have to travel longer distances, nature slows maturity one year to give them time to get there. Then, when the young have been spawned, each little eel starts back to the precise river its mother started from the year before. One never sees a European eel in American rivers nor an American eel in European waters.

What is this mystery, this wisdom, this foreknowledge operating in the lowest creatures? It is beyond the comprehension of the scientist, who can only record it as a phenomenon, but can never explain what it is or why it occurs. But it certainly is intelligent action above that of bee, bug, or eel. The lower universe is evidently indwelt by something from the higher.

THE "IMPOSSIBLE"

He who says that anything is impossible forgets the scope of the Intelligent Power whose silent guiding activities are evident in the field of both inorganic and living form. Is it reasonable, therefore, to suppose that man alone is exempt from this quiet brooding Presence? It is pessimism to take this stand.

True optimism boldly avers that Infinite Intelligence will have at least as much interest in a man as in a bee or a beetle. There must be and there is a solution to that seemingly insurmountable financial or health problem. There is a Power and a Wisdom available for man in his deepest crisis. Upon this the optimist draws.

True optimism, then, is not a fatuous smile, a weak Pollyanna philosophy, a "keep smiling" attitude. It is a well-thought-out thought-pattern, based upon clear and indisputable evidence, which dares to go beyond the timidity of those afraid of being "unscientific" if they mention God's nearness to man; and the true optimist draws healing into his body or those of others by the positiveness of his attitudes.

The wonders of the universe have only been

scratched. Today man is only in the kindergarten stage playing with the little building blocks of the universe. Tomorrow he will put away childish things and will penetrate the great mysteries of his spiritual inheritance, for this field is the advanced university of life.

Even now we do not understand the mystery of breathing, and we knew less when we were born. Yet we breathed in that first moment of life, and we are breathing now. We do not always need to understand a mystery in order to experience it.

In the movement of Infinite Life we recognize something which is far beyond the loftiest human comprehension. We would not presume to describe God, for we know so little about Him. But this much we have learned, that he who drops his hatreds, envies, bitter resentments, jealousies, fears, and anxieties, and who dares to believe that the indescribable Healing Presence flows through him can be healed and is being healed, for there is definite healing force in this sort of optimism.

Chapter II

THE HEALING POWER OF BALANCED EMOTIONS

PERHAPS the greatest compliment we can pay another is to say, "He is well balanced." Yet it is not always easy to define the term. Dr. Flanders Dunbar, one of the outstanding authorities in the field of psychosomatic medicine, has said that balanced emotions produce a personality (1) that is unhampered by mental conflict (2) that has a satisfactory work capacity (3) which gets along well with others.

Most of us have certain points at which we are off balance to a certain degree. Perhaps these slight imbalances will always be with us. They are occasions for alarm only when they hold us in mental conflict, prevent our doing satisfactory work, keep us from getting along well with others, or cause physical illness.

The well-balanced personality is a mixture of the masculine and the feminine. A man should be about eighty per cent masculine with an admixture of twenty per cent feminine; a woman should be eighty per cent feminine and twenty per cent masculine.

The shaggy-chested man beating his way through life and crushing everyone else to the side may think of himself as a "he-man"; but he will not be a complete, well-balanced personality until he has acquired that twenty per cent of tenderness, understanding, and sympathy for others. On the other hand, the woman who is completely a clinging vine, with no mind of her own, may imagine herself to be truly feminine; but she is not truly feminine until she possesses that twenty per cent of initiative, originality, and independent thought and opinion usually associated with the masculine.

The balanced personality always maintains equilibrium between a normal, rational self-interest and an inordinate selfishness which continues to place himself at the center of life. He does not take unfair advantage of others. He does not allow others to take advantage of him.

The extreme introvert and the extreme extrovert are both unbalanced. There is a pleasant balance between extroversion and introversion which makes for an excellent state of harmony.

One needs a combination of prudence and courage in approaching life; there is a sensible prudence which is a moderate fear coupled with a particular kind of courage which dares to take a risk when that seems necessary. The truly balanced person has a certain amount of meekness coupled with an equal aggressiveness, a modest refinement untainted by prudery.

Some are completely absorbed in material things. They deal in facts, figures, and business statistics. They have the false notion that all success is measured in terms of money or possessions. These are as one-sided as the hermit who renounces all material possessions. Both hermit and extreme materialist are unbalanced.

THE BODY REFLECTS EMOTIONAL BALANCE

Naturally enough, when one's personality is out of balance, he will usually find his body veering into a corresponding distortion, for illness is the imbalance of thought reproducing itself in body tissues.

Sometimes the individual will claim that it is his duty to immerse himself in a one-sided view of life, but his body does not care whether it is his "duty" or not, for the body is naturally characterized by the same hidden rhythms that are found throughout the universe. Nothing is out of balance anywhere in the universe; the periodic rhythms seen throughout all nature are reflected in the human body.

When man balances his mental, emotional, and spiritual patterns in rhythm, balance, order, and regularity, his body automatically responds; his new attitudes toward life in general result in balancing the endocrine glands, the blood, the digestive organs, and all the other components of the body.

Since the rise of psychosomatic medicine, there has been a decided shift in the doctor's approach to his patients. Years ago his approach was based on a "cellular pathology," which dealt with the individual diseased cell. Today the term used is "organismal pathology," which considers the organism as a whole, meaning that when the body is ill, the whole man is ill. Dr. Dunbar asserts that a person's lungs, heart, business, love affairs, hatreds, and grudges are all related aspects of one organism, and that when one part is ill, the rest of the organism reflects this illness, hence the term, "psychosomatic," from the Greek "psyche" (mind) and "soma" (body). It is impossible to tell where body leaves off and mind begins, for the two are inextricably interwoven. Balanced emotions mean a balanced body.

This might appear to be a very advanced position; in reality it has been well known to the seers of all ages. Jesus taught that the law of balance, rhythm, harmony, which he called Love, is the fundamental of man's existence. He advised his hearers to seek this above everything. He called it the Kingdom of God, and he admonished them not to look for it anywhere else but within themselves. He taught that when man learns to balance himself in his relationship to the Infinite, his physical disorders will become things of the past.

Otherwise, he will be treating as a unit that which is only a symptom of a larger unit, which is the organism as a whole; and he will be disappointed at its apparent incurability. In reality, there are no incurable conditions; there are only incomplete approaches which never reach the real seat of the trouble, unbalanced emotions.

THE HEALING POWER PROVED IN ACTUAL CASES

The healing power of balanced emotions has been vividly demonstrated in the lives of several prominent persons.

Elizabeth Barrett Browning was one of a large family ruled over by a tyrannical despot of a father, who shut them away from outside companionship, fiercely jealous of their love. As a young woman, Elizabeth took to her bed following an accident from which she should have quickly recovered. But this was her unconscious retreat from the impact of her father's dictatorship. In her room, she could roam the centuries, cultivating those heroes of ancient Greece, pouring out her confused emotions in verse.

One volume of her poem was read by Robert Browning. He wrote her his appreciation; after several months' correspondence he came to see her during her father's absence. Their love grew—the only love she had ever known. She was almost forty, an invalid, with a father who would have physically thrown the young Browning out if he had known he was visiting her, for he had done this to another young man years before.

But love triumphed. Its balancing effect obliterated the destructive effects of her previously unbalanced emotions. She rose from the invalid's bed; they eloped. She became an active mountain climber in Europe, where they spent several years. At forty-three she gave birth to a fine son. Her whole being had become integrated under the healing power of balanced emotions.

Nathaniel Hawthorne and Sophia Peabody had a somewhat similar experience. Nathaniel had been reared in a dark, gloomy mansion. The children were seldom allowed outside, and never had visitors. A brilliant student and gifted writer, he moved through life apart, as though afraid of mankind. Sophia had been badly injured; the tragic experience had left her a nervous wreck with recurrent spasms of agony. She was almost helpless physically. Hawthorne and Sophia fell in love. Everyone advised against the marriage of this thirty-eight-year-old introvert and the physically incapable invalid.

Then Sophia took the somewhat primitive position that if God wanted her to marry, He would heal her. It is not known exactly which steps she took in her mental rightabout-face, but whatever path she followed resulted in the integrating of her emotional life, and in her newly balanced emotions she found complete healing. She brought to Hawthorne the only substantial joy he was ever to know in life, and proved herself a tower of strength to him in crisis. They and their children were a most happy family.

We do not always realize how deeply the things that we love or hate enter into the actual composition of our bodies. Both Sophia Peabody and Elizabeth Barrett were consumed by unconscious hate, which is only the reverse side of fear. Where hate is dominant, the body must reflect that dominance in its functioning. But when love replaces hate, the emotions are now balanced, and the body just as readily reflects the new attitude.

THE ACCIDENT-PRONE PERSON'S EMOTIONS

Dr. Dunbar tells of a young man, one of a family of nineteen children. He had always hated his father because of the merciless thrashings received from him. When he was a child, nobody had ever given him love, for his mother always had another small child or two to look after. He had thought that all families were like his own; therefore he never had demanded love. But the natural hunger for love was an unconscious craving deep within him.

He had been a carpenter, truck driver, and professional boxer. He was by no means the "sissy" type. But some years before, he had broken his arm. In the hospital he had received personal attention such as he had never enjoyed before. It awoke in him that for which he had been craving unconsciously. When Dunbar's assistants came across him, he had broken bones several times during the past few years. He had not deliberately tried to receive fractures. It was an entirely unconscious operation, in which his craving for love and attention set the stage for the accident which would bring him to the hospital where his deeper hungers for attention would be met.

When this was pointed out to him, and he was shown how he could draw to himself those emotional satisfactions he needed, there were no more accidents.

A significant theory grew from Dr. Dunbar's diagnosis of his case. It has been discovered that there are "accident-prone" persons, who unconsciously attract accidents to themselves in order to escape from something else. They do not realize that they have hidden emotional conflicts; they think that they are just "unlucky." But a study of their mental processes reveals the true cause of their trouble to a skilled observer like Dr. Dunbar.

Such illustrations are found by the hundred in the writings of those who are practicing psychosomatic medicine. They bear out the fact that even the repeated business failures of a person are traceable to an unconscious desire to punish either himself or others for some imagined infractions of the rules of life. Our minds are curiously complex, and do not always reveal the true motives for our behavior, but our unbalanced emotions are behind every unhappy moment we experience.

EXCESSIVE DRINKING BASED IN EMOTIONAL IMBALANCE

Drs. Haggard and Jellinek, of Yale University, have made exhaustive studies into the deep underlying causes of excessive drinking. Accordingly they divide problem drinkers into four types.

The understanding person never condemns the excessive drinker, for he is not an individual determined to wreck society or to destroy his family's happiness. He is an emotionally ill person, and can be freed when his emotions are once more set in balance. If this is not done, all the chemical "cures" on earth will not free him from his habit, for it is fundamentally emotional, not physical. Once he is emotionally freed, the very desire for liquor fades away, and there is no necessity for gritting his teeth and fighting it desperately. In fact, as long as this latter seems necessary, it is an indication that he has not yet arrived at the real source of his difficulty, which is not a weak will but unbalanced emotional patterns.

Jellinek and Haggard's four types are as follows: first, the symptomatic drinker. This is one in whom his indulgence is a symptom of definite psychosis. He might be either a manic depressive or a dementia praecox. His drinking might be a concomitant of epilepsy.

The second type is rather foolish, for he is of the opinion that it is necessary to drink in order to stay in with the crowd he admires. As an adolescent he drinks to prove his manhood.

The third type starts drinking normally in a social way, then discovers that when he is faced with a problem, he seems to face it better if he has a few drinks. The habit grows on him from a mental and emotional cause rather than from a physical craving for liquor as a drink. It is a retreat from the ugly or difficult things of life. He really wishes to be anesthetized to his problems.

Fourthly, there is the neurotic drinker. According to Haggard and Jellinek, he is the most difficult to reach. His drinking is part of a deep personality problem. There is usually evidence of a great sense of frustration or loss. Perhaps there was great ambition with subsequent failure to realize his goal.

Perhaps he greatly underestimates his own ability, for often he is a person of high capability but accompanied by an inferiority complex.

These researchers have shown that there is nothing physical within the person which actually craves or demands alcohol. The whole "need" is mental from beginning to end. The reserved person finds alcohol producing a feeling of camaraderie impossible when sober. It stirs up the feeling that he can "tell anybody off," even the police officer or the boss. It gives him "Dutch courage." He is no longer timid; he can voice his views in any company, or approach persons difficult to approach when he is sober. He can become "the life of the party" and enjoy the limelight.

MIND POSSESSES ALL POWER

The healing of the alcoholic problem depends upon an intelligent approach. Alcohol of itself has no power to impart qualities or capabilities. It may release powers deeply buried, but these abilities must be there originally or barrels of liquor could not bring them into existence.

Therefore the intelligent person knows that his mind, within itself, possesses the power to be unafraid of others, to talk easily and freely in company, to approach difficult persons, or to have that true feeling of camaraderie. Therefore, sober, he must have been living below his own true self, and the drinks have only removed the barriers of his repression for the time being. In other words, he has always had as much freedom as the most courageous person, but he has been stifling it.

MIND CAN RELEASE ITS OWN POWER

If the mind can thus be liberated temporarily through liquor, it must be possible to bring it to the same level without alcohol. Millions of non-drinkers do this.

They have learned to have a true regard for themselves; they are conscious of their own manhood or womanhood, and don't need drinks to bring it to the fore. They know quietly within themselves that they can meet and face any situation clear-eyed, because there is something within them which is greater than anything that can ever come against them. Within themselves they are secure and confident, and they don't very much care whether others know it or not.

They certainly are not going to lift a glass to prove it or to gain the approbation of others, for this would be placing themselves beneath those whose good opinion they court. They try to be all of themselves at every point, and they will not try to be more of themselves by being less of themselves. What they think of themselves is more important to them than what others think of them, and they know that man's true status is far above any level reached in a stupefied condition.

MAN'S MIND AN EXTENSION OF THE INFINITE

In the Science of Mind we take the individual onto a higher level than psychosomatic medicine or psychiatry does. We believe that his mind is only an extension of the Infinite Mind operating within a human frame, limited only by human beliefs.

This Intelligence is never bound by any hostile or opposing power. It is always in perfect equilibrium, because its beliefs are always perfectly balanced.

Man is made in this same image and likeness; therefore, basically he is as free and balanced as the Infinite Intelligence. But in experience his beliefs are distorted; therefore, he is bound in chains. But these chains are of his own making, for they are the outcome of his beliefs about himself and about his helplessness. His bondage is not to something external like alcohol but to his internal belief that liquor has some diabolical power over him.

This belief is based upon a deeper false belief that the world is against him, or that he has failed to achieve a goal, or has suffered irreparable loss, or is baffled and frustrated. The underlying belief usually contains some element of self-pity or guilt, and the drinking either feeds or mollifies that element.

When he is led to see that the crux of the problem is his relationship to the Infinite, he now holds the key to his freedom within his hands. When he believes that whatever is true of the Infinite must of necessity be true of him, he rises to a transcendent position where he lives far above frustration, disappointment, self-pity, fear of the opinions of others; and with this new concept of himself there is no desire to run away, for there is no longer anything to run away from.

Thus there is no longer any necessity to take the narcotic which leads him into a false security, and the so-called appetite for liquor passes away. It never was a true appetite; it was only the symptom of a hunger for mastery of life, which it seemed to furnish; and it was the only answer he knew to the unappeasable hunger for union with his Source, with its accompanying sense of mastery and "worthwhileness."

The excessive drinker is what he is because of unbalanced emotions. His healing can come only through their re-balancing. This comes through his understanding of his true nature, his manhood, and his inherent powers; and no better way has yet been found to do this than by the realization that man is a spiritual being united at his deepest center with That which is never bound nor limited, partaking of God's qualities because his own mind is merely the mind of God encased in a human form.

This does not mean that man must become an evangelist or a theologian. Some do, to their great credit. It does not mean that he must become sanctimonious, or be any less masculine than he has been. It does not necessarily mean that he join a church, or attend one, although he will be wise if he affiliates with a church whose teachings are based upon sound, constructive principles of modern thinking. Many persons shrink from "God" associations because their memories of such call up pictures of an unreal, sanctimonious, or hypocritical nature, in which they were scared into an external goodness by the threat of hell fire. This is an entirely erroneous picture.

THE "GODLY" MAN

A "godly" man is merely one who endeavors to reproduce within himself the nature of God. Honor, honesty, justice to others, good will to all, coupled with a sense of inner adequacy which gives him the quiet confidence that he can meet life at any point—these are the qualities of the "godly" man. A recognition of the tremendous force of inward spiritual power and the assurance that he is always in touch with it is the perfect foundation for the balancing of emotions.

Those who are thus healed are in one sense "new men." "Old things have passed away. All things have become new." This is why the person who is healed through a sane, well-balanced understanding of spiritual things usually becomes far more successful in business; for the fundamental principles of successful living are likewise those of successful business. The same principle that heals a sick business heals a sick body or a sick personality. Life is complex, but basically it is far simpler than most of us realize. There is far-reaching power to heal in balanced emotions.

Chapter III

THE HEALING POWER OF THE IMAGINATION

THE MOMENT we mention the imagination in relation to healing, we run into difficulty, for the picture called up is that of an excitable person who imagines he is seriously ill because he has a pain. Then someone comes along and changes the picture by switching his mind in the opposite direction so that he now imagines he does not have the illness any more, and the whole procedure has been one of self-hypnosis. Our use of the word "imagination" has nothing to do with such highly hysterical contortions. We use it in its basic meaning, which is the power to image.

One Sunday morning following our service, a woman aproached me and explained that she was a registered nurse. She had been assigned to a case several months previously. Her patient was a highly educated man, formerly a university professor. He was blind in one eye, and the sight of the other was almost gone. His doctor had told him that he could not expect any improvement in his condition; so one day early in their association she had asked him what he thought of the possibility of mental and spiritual healing. His reply was, "Nobody but a crackpot would expect to be healed that way. It's all imagination from beginning to end." To him it was completely unscientific, absurd, ridiculous.

One evening she was in her room with the radio turned low, listening to one of our programs. He caught snatches of it from time to time. Next morning he asked what the program had been, saying that he had enjoyed the little he had heard. He began tuning it in, and ultimately it got to the point where he would allow nothing to interfere with his hearing that broadcast.

Evidently he was doing more than listening. He must have been absorbing ideas, for within a few months his eyesight had recovered to such a degree that he had now started on a trip to the east coast, driving his own car, something completely beyond the bounds of possibility a few months earlier.

A person who has placed terms such as "spiritual healing" or "imagination" in a certain connotation finds it difficult to divorce himself from that understanding of the word. The student of semantics knows that one must separate words from their previous connotations to gain their true meaning and implications.

IMAGINATION IN THE PROGRESS OF THE RACE

Far from being of low estimation, the imagination is one of the most important constituents of man's mentality. It must have come before reason in his mental development, and, therefore, exercises greater power than reason in determining the conduct of most people. Where the will and the imagination come into conflict, the imagination usually wins.

All the progress of the race has come from the exercise of the imagination. The individual who could never see anything better than he had could never see anything toward which he could or should advance. The true benefactors of the race were those who could envision a better way of doing things; this is the true use of imagination, the process of imaging. From it have come all invention, art, music, ideals, the growth of business and industry, in fact, civilization.

Man's language, both spoken and written, is the product of imagination. Animals have sounds to express various moods, such as alarm, rage, fear, and tenderness. Man has expanded these sounds into exact words which express shades of meaning. Words are symbols of things which man's imagination has invented. They denote a certain creativeness.

In fact, the first language man used was that of poetry. The word "poet" denotes a maker, a creator. The first language took words rich in emotional significance and expressed them in poetic form. Carlyle asked, "Do you think that there were not poets before Chaucer?" He knew that far back, even before Virgil and Homer, the first man who ever expressed words must have lifted himself beyond the immediate and spoken of that which was only a mental picture at the time.

True, the Homeric poems were the language of an exalted soul soaring far beyond the experiences of the earth, describing experiences which transcend those of the ordinary man, using word-symbols rich and warm in feeling, which have since filtered down into everyday usage, but originally being products entirely of an exalted imagination. They may have lost their fine poetic warmth and have become commonplace, but originally all words were highly imaginative.

Each idea and experience that man works out in action is the product of imagination, because it has been preceded by a specific concept. Those who advance beyond their neighbors in individual achievement have done so through their use of a highly developed creative imagination. No one has ever succeeded unless he has exercised imagination beyond that of his fellows.

IMAGINATION AND SCIENCE

Some scientists say that they forswear the use of imagination and deal only with demonstrable facts and figures. A little thought will show that this is not so. All our great scientific advances have been merely the outreaching of minds not satisfied with the story the facts and figures have told. All the facts concerning falling apples were known to the scientists of Newton's day; yet only he had the imaginative activity to formulate the correct hypothesis and to prove it. At every stage of scientific advance, there has been a man of imagination.

The ordinary scientist is really nothing more than a fact-stuffer. He assembles the facts and tells what they are; he may make a deduction within the facts, or parrot the conclusions already made by others. But the true scientist assembles the same facts, lays them out upon another platform, views them from an entirely different angle, blazes a new trail in the field of knowledge, and proves a new theory.

A scientist without creative imagination is not a true scientist at all; he is only a fact-assembling hack. The true scientist is as much an artist as he who creates with oils, brush, and palette; the only difference is that he works with mathematics and test tube.

IMAGINATION AND INVENTION

Imagination is the creative tool of inventors. They are not dreamy, visionary, useless, impractical, theoretical drifters. The practical inventor uses his imagination to see beyond the level of our present achievement, then adds his creative ability to bring into being a new gadget that works better than that which has been. Like Edison, he might have to conduct hundreds or thousands of experiments before his practical imagination can be made to coincide with his dream, but when the final experiment is successful, it is his imagination that has triumphed.

IMAGINATION AND DIFFICULTIES

Those who give up in the face of difficulties are lacking in imagination. For the same reason, many remain ill when they could be completely well. Two persons are confronted with the same sort of barrier. One stops, tries feebly, and gives up. The other says. "There must be some way around, over, or through this barrier." But no way is apparent; it seems hopeless, as it did to the first person.

This is where we all stand at the parting of the ways. The same appearances, the same facts, the same sort of situation. With this difference! One is too lethargic or too easily discouraged to call upon his imagination. The other is not!

When Admiral Peary was a young man he dreamed of making his way one day to the North Pole. His instructors in naval college said. "There is no way." During his naval career he often spoke of it. Everyone said, "There is no way." This had stopped all others in the past. But Peary turned his face away from what his eyes could see and his ears hear, away from the visible impossibilities, and turning inward upon his imagination he said, "I will find a way or make one." This became his slogan. After he had started on his perilous journey, when lost, cold, and hungry, he sent men back, he pushed on, muttering through clenched teeth, "I will find a way or make one." And imagination made a way.

A young man was incarcerated in San Quentin prison. He allowed himself to become neither bitter nor hopeless. With time on his hands, he figured out an entirely new method of merchandising. Upon his release, he started a store based upon the product of his imagination; it grew into a vast chain, which he sold out for seven figures. He was a poet-creator just as truly as if he had been painting a mural.

All good businessmen are poet-creators. So is every person who steps ahead of the crowd.

There was a woman who made good money all through the depression. She would look at a house that was almost tumbling down, buy and remodel it, and take her profit, all this on very limited capital at first. When I spoke about it, she said, "I see possibilities in them." Notice that phrase, "I see possibilities in them." Thousands of persons walking that street had said, "What an eyesore! Why don't they condemn it?" They saw it *with* their eyes, and all they saw were the visible facts. It was an eyesore. She looked at the same house *through* her eyes, and her imagination drew the picture of the house it could be.

When the eyes of the imagination are opened, any condition can be changed and results produced which are impossible to him who "has eyes to see but does not see."

If we have normal sympathies, we are bound to feel pity for the person who has never had a chance. Yet we must remember that in the ranks of the "underprivileged," reared in the same alley in the same slums, seeing the same conduct and hearing the same criminal conversations, was someone who never allowed the slum to put its measure upon him. Shaking free from the defeated talk, putting his imagination to work, he has said, "I will find a way or make one." Soon he is no longer in the slum. He was underprivileged as long as his imagination remained unaroused. When he allowed it to become active, he conceived a better level of living.

No person can remain underprivileged when he dares to follow his imagination. He knows that external betterment bestowed upon those who remain unimaginative is soon dragged down to a low level and nothing has been permanently benefited.

A great detective takes a torn scrap of paper neglected by the ordinary officer investigating the crime. He allows his imagination to operate upon this jagged piece of paper, filling in hypothetical reasons why it was found at the scene of the crime, until step by step his creative imagination traces it to the guilty person. The unimaginative officer cannot understand why the great detective is so "lucky."

The anthropologist can take a portion of the skull of a man who lived a quarter of a million years ago; through his imagination he rebuilds it until he can tell us the characteristics of the man, the level of his reasoning powers and of his ideals, the extent of his speech faculty, and the degree of memory the man must have possessed. The scientist can take one bone covered with the silt and ashes of the ages and can reconstruct the dinosaur or the sabre-toothed tiger, telling us of its dietary and other living habits.

The astrophysicist can roam through space in his disciplined imagination. His high-powered lens tells us much about the distant worlds which shine like pinpoints in the night sky. The imagination checks through the spectroscope and tells us the constituents of that star, the atmosphere surrounding it, and a myriad facts concerning its distance, speed, and size.

We repeat, man's imagination is the faculty that has led him onward, ever climbing to higher levels of achievement and of living. It is now being called upon to free him from illness. But we must see it as a helper and friend, not as a hindrance; and it must be disciplined.

IMAGINATION MUST BE CULTIVATED

Each of us has imagination, even he who says, "Oh, I have no imagination at all." But it atrophies when allowed to fall into disuse. Then it appears to be nonexistent. But brought back into activity, it will live, grow and expand. He who begins once more to cultivate it will find that it responds beautifully to use, and will furnish him with creative ideas that seem to come from nowhere.

Goethe said that if one wants to develop the aesthetic sense, he should hang a beautiful work of art upon the wall of a much-used room; then seeing this essential beauty consciously and unconsciously as he passes it each day, he will inevitably draw to himself that inner standard of beauty which the work of art represents. In consequence, his ability to appreciate and appraise art and beauty will be raised to a higher degree.

This is true of the imagination. The individual who cultivates the ability to see, not *with* his eyes but *through* his eyes, will find these inner eyes penetrating the dense veil of the material which hides so much of the realities of life from many. He will find himself moving into realms in which the things that used to be "imaginary" become vested with the deepest reality. Then the reality of life begins to operate upon him; for we do not operate on life; it operates upon us and through us.

IMAGINATION MUST BE DISCIPLINED

But the problem arises concerning the wrong use of the imagination. Every fear that has ever bedeviled man is a wrong use of the imagination. Wrongly used, this faculty can build up menacing pictures, ugly suspicions, green-eyed jealousies, searing resentments, and debilitating self-pity. These lock us within a prison of our own thinking while they emerge in the form of various illnesses.

Psychosomatic medicine has shown that much arthritis in later years is the outgrowth of bitterness and resentment long carried, either secretly or openly. Resentment is the result of a misreading of life and of a misunderstanding of the forces which play upon us. He who sees life clearly knows that nothing ever done to him or said about him can hurt him without his own consent. Moreover, he knows that the normal, well-balanced person never deliberately does a mean, cutting thing. So he concludes that the person who has wronged him must be a warped, deformed, unbalanced character.

Knowing these things, he cannot feel resentment. Instead, a sense of pity coupled with deep gratitude steals into his heart—pity for the poor misshapen personality that tried to hurt him, gratitude for the fact that he himself is normal enough not to find it necessary to drop to the level of hatred.

When life attains that level in which we look *through* the eyes rather than *with* the eyes, we no longer see enemies. We look through the twisted exterior of those who think they are our enemies, and we see their hurt, starved souls blindly lashing out to allay their own inner hurt, and pity wipes out resentment. The only hurts they can inflict upon us are the hurts we create within ourselves by dwelling upon the supposed unfairness of their treatment of us.

When we see life in proper perspective, we recognize that our so-called enemy is only the product of his environment. The influences that have played upon him since childhood have warped him. If we had grown up under the same influences, we should have been just as warped and mean as he is now. If he had been subjected to the same environmental conditions with which we have been favored, he would be as we are today. Our gratitude, therefore, blots out any incipient resentment through the constructive use of the imagination.

All the misunderstandings of life are the product of a wrongly used imagination. Man can use this excellent faculty for good or evil. He can accept life's affronts, or he can turn them into steppingstones to greater peace of mind and better health. The imagination is the servant; it can be turned in whatever direction each chooses. It is by no means master, except where one fails to train it constructively.

Applied to the healing of the body in this scientific manner, it is most certainly not what the professor thought only a bunch of crackpots believed in. It is the most powerful restorer to health known; yet, used destructively, it can destroy the body.

IMAGINATION USED FOR GOOD OR ILL

Two patients may be presented with a similar diagnosis. The prognosis is not good. The doctor admits that the condition is grave. He may say that he doubts that anything can be done for either of them.

One immediately uses his imagination to recall some friend who was told the same thing, and who passed away within a short time. His imagination accentuates slight symptoms, making him think his heart is pounding harder than it is, or that physical distress or weakness is more pronounced than it is. He is helpless in an emotional typhoon, carried along feebly on the gales of fear. He becomes panicky, desperate. The tides of morbid feeling rise higher and higher within him. He takes to feeling his pulse and examining his tongue.

After all, the doctor's prognosis might not have been strictly true. The condition might not have been so desperate as he assumed. But this type of patient often passes on, killed by his fear, which is only another term for a destructive use of the imagination.

The second patient gets hold of himself. He has as much reason for becoming panicky, but he inhibits the rising storm through constructive use of the imagination. He tells himself that many patients have attended the funeral of the doctor who had condemned them to death. He realizes that if he cannot detach himself from the actual condition, at least he can free himself from the fear of the condition.

He holds himself steady, searches the halls of memory for similar cases where the person recovered his health. If he does not know of them personally, he reads the literature of spiritual healing and learns how common such healings are. If people ask how he is, he tells them he is feeling better. He ignores the temporary spells as far as he can, and he centers his thought upon a Power so great as to be resistless. He invites this Power to operate within him. He looks eagerly for any sign of improvement. He cultivates the cheerful, constructive attitudes and does his best to turn away from the doleful.

He recovers and lives, for there is tremendous healing power in the imagination, scientifically used.

We are not subbornly dogmatic, because there is much about the intricacies of man's mind which is not fully understood, but we venture the opinion that these healings take place because our imagination is that of the Infinite Intelligence.

The universe has not existed eternally; therefore, there must have been a time when there was only Intelligence and—nothing. The God-Mind imaged a universe and brought it into being. Since all matter in the universe is basically one substance, so it is reasonable to assume that all Intelligence is one.

If this be so, then what we call our "imagination" is merely the streaming through us of that Infinite faculty which brought the universe into form. Naturally it is modified by the human vehicle through which it operates, but basically it is the same, and the more closely we can approximate our employment of it to the way the Infinite employs it, the more truly will it reproduce its beneficial effects within our bodies. To the degree that we can detach ourselves from our fear and allow our imagination to move with its true Source, we shall find our healing.

Some will immediately forsake all material assistance. Others, reluctant to make such a drastic move, will continue with their medicine or diet or manipulations.

But whatever we do from the physical side, we shall rise in our thought to its highest possible level, and will use our constructive imagination to picture ourselves constantly as the Source is, and as the Infinite sees us to be, perfect, without weakness at any point. As the Source is continually conscious of its infinite resources, so we shall know that this force in us has ample resources to build as many new healthy cells as are necessary and to restore perfect balance in every part.

It is quite possible for one to walk with his head in the clouds, but the well-balanced person keeps his feet on the ground at the same time. Man walks the earthly path of his material life, but he now enters upon that inward spiritual path, guided by his constructive imagination.

When he walks this double path, he draws constantly from the spiritual world and allows this spiritual force to permeate all his earthly activities. Colored now by his constructive imagination, his whole life takes on new meaning. Mystery and hocus-pocus pass out of his life. He finds himself on sound foundations under the resistless healing power of the imagination.

Chapter IV

THE HEALING POWER OF FAITH

OUR NEXT approach to healing is through faith. I shall bring in a personal experience at this point, as it seems to furnish an apt starting point.

When I was twenty-six years of age, my whole world came tumbling down around my ears. I had spent many difficult years in institutions of higher learning preparing myself for my life's work and was rejoicing in the fact that my final year's training in a London hospital was almost over. Then I was going to Bolivia to set up and operate a hospital for a missionary society among the Indians.

During the last week of my training, it was discovered that I was suffering from diabetes. Insulin had not then been discovered, and it was a death sentence for any young person who contracted it. Two famous physicians knew me well enough to tell me the truth, which was that I had less than two years to live. It was a body blow. I felt hopeless, confused, and bitter.

After about six weeks of bewilderment, I was brought into contact with a new idea through the writings of Thomas Troward, one of the most penetrating thinkers of this century. Troward's principal thesis is that the individual can create for himself any new condition he desires if he learns how to align his thinking with that of the Infinite, because man's ability to create new conditions follows the same sequences which the Creator used in bringing the universe into existence; that is, there is a *creative process in the individual.*

It was a startling concept, but it gave promise of at least a chance for life. Like a drowning man clutching at a straw, I grasped at it, with the result that these many years later I am teaching this method of healing and helping others find the pathway to health. When I say that there are no incurable illnesses, my conclusion is based not alone on my personal experience but upon those of tens of thousands in whom this resistless tide of healing has flowed.

The hopeless, desolate individual who has been told that nothing more can be done for him should be reminded that the human mind has vast unexplored territory in which lie tremendous resources for healing. His mind is actually an extension of the Infinite Mind. This is not just a pretty figure of speech; it is actual fact. But man usually has to come to the limit of human resources before he will dare to launch himself upon that illimitable ocean of the Infinite. When he does so, he finds that "with God all things are possible."

WHAT FAITH IS AND IS NOT

Since this chapter deals with the healing power of faith, we should have a clear understanding of what faith is and what it is not. Faith is not blind credulity. By training and natural inclination, I demand reasonable proof before taking any stand. My feet must stand on a solid foundation.

I want the same sort of faith that underlies the activities of Drs. Dunbar, Weiss, English, Cannon, Carrel, Hinsey, and others who have been trained in logical scientific methods, and who, by following their own clear discriminative powers of observation, have come to the conclusion that the key to man's healing lies buried within his own mind. They see a tremendous force acting through man's thought-life. Whether they speak of this as God is not important. They all recognize that it has distinct power to alter physical tissue and restore health.

There is a certain type which can be excited into a sort of faith on an air-bubble foundation of feeling, but the faith that is solid and substantial is built upon logical premises and conclusions. In the Science of Mind, we recognize universal law as operating upon three levels. The scientist deals with those unalterable physical laws which govern the activity of matter. The psychologist works with those mental laws which operate in the field of mind. But the spiritual scientist recognizes the existence of a third tier of laws which operate in man's distinctly spiritual nature.

A person could live like an animal through physical law only, gratifying his appetites, caring for little else. Some people live on this level. He could add the mental interests, thereby rising to a more permanent and satisfactory level of life. But no one can experience the reality of God and the spiritual forces until he recognizes the existence of spiritual law.

It is in this particular field that we operate. We do not ignore physical and mental law. They have their legitimate place in man's life, and their practice by the various schools of healing has been of inestimable benefit to the race. But even while we are encouraging men to revise their thought patterns in line with mental law, our faith is not in this revision but in the spiritual incoming of a distinctly spiritual power.

Wars have been fought and men burned at the stake in an effort to define this spiritual power. For convenience we use the terms "God," "The Infinite Intelligence," "Divine Mind." The name does not matter much, although some literal-minded persons are highly incensed when we use the second or third term. The important thing is to establish contact with it. We use the pronouns "He" or "It" interchangeably. Those who insist upon "He" have never satisfactorily shown why a bodiless spiritual principle has to be male.

In spiritual faith, we go much further than either the material healer or the psychosomaticist. It is our belief that the physical is the broad base of a cone; the mental is the middle section. These two leave us with an incomplete, truncated cone. It requires the recognition of the spiritual to draw that cone to its natural fine point. This latter we add.

The former two can be contacted and recognized through sight and reason. The third section is made operative through a fine, intangible. spiritual perception, which sees the visible form as a transitory covering house in which man, the permanent, dwells. The laws of this inner dweller are those of love, quiet assurance, perfection, practiced not to produce union with God, but as a result of union with Him. It is a matter of the Infinite reproducing in man that which God is in Himself as a result of a certain relationship that man has established.

Thus, it is a notable fact that when a person's body has been healed by spiritual means, that person is never the same person again. He finds a spiritual law written on his heart rather than imposed from without. This law lifts him onto a higher vantage point; he sees life, as it were, from an eminence; he sees the great mass of struggling, greedy, burdened humanity, staggering under a great load of false belief which reflects itself in their illnesses and defeats. He becomes gentler in his understanding of their meannesses, tolerant of their weaknesses. Resentments and desire for revenge pass away.

This is not so much a conscious, deliberate program on his part; it is as though life from another world had touched him. He is new born. Perhaps this was what was meant by the words: "If any man be in Christ, he is a new creature." It is a spiritual rather than a mental experience, difficult to explain in cold type. But it is real—in fact, the most real experience of his whole life. It is his introduction to *spiritual* reality.

THE HEALING POWER OF FAITH PROVED

Five years ago, a woman was told that she was in a precarious condition with enlarged heart, leaking valves, and a blood pressure of two hundred and sixty. When seen again a few months ago, she was the picture of health. Her scope of vision had been broadened to include not only heart and arteries but the entire world. She confessed that she had been a most disagreeable shopper, and that her friends and relatives had found her most difficult. "Now," she said, "I have discovered that the way I regard my maid, the grocer's clerk, and all those I meet has been completely reversed."

It has been said. "Whatsoever ye believe, it is done unto you." This is to say, our mental patterns are the mosaic of our inner life, including everything we think and all the attitudes we take. We may think they are far removed from the physical organism; yet they are tied directly to it, and are part of it.

This woman said that since now she regards the world and its people as part of herself, there is an unforced graciousness apparent in her. She no longer feels that she is being pulled apart. Instead, life in all its parts now forms one complete harmonious pattern. She is one with the whole.

The physical result of this new faith is that the body tissues have responded to the balanced ease of her thinking, and her healing has come. This is because man thinks, not alone with his brain or mind, but with every cell of his body. The new faith engendered in this woman is sending a new quality of nerve energy to every cell, harmony has replaced discord, and it is being done unto her according to her new belief.

OUR BELIEFS EXTERNALIZE

That which we believe about life, the universe, other persons, ourselves, or the Infinite will be manifested in our bodies. It can not be otherwise, for "men can not gather grapes from thorns, nor figs from thistles."

We are sometimes astounded to find that the condition we had thought to be completely physical is almost completely mental and spiritual. It is our distorted thought appearing in form. The outer disturbance is merely the visible sign of inward disturbance.

Conversely, when the inward picture changes, the outer follows. There is nothing mysterious about it; it is a straight working of cause and effect. The deep interior causes of either illness or health lie hidden within the recesses of the human mind.

This new view brings the person to see that the universal Intelligence is not hostile but friendly, and he will not misunderstand its action. Our close friends can say things to us that strangers could never say, and we do not misunderstand them; we know that they could not possibly mean anything hostile because we are certain of their friendship toward us. When we come to know that the universal Intelligence is friendly, we know that it could never wish illness or suffering upon us in an arbitrary way. Sickness is an out-and-out effect of a cause which arises within our own thought.

FAITH IN THE UNCHANGING REAL

The widow of a prominent man had been told that she had a malignant condition. She had learned the difference between the changing unreal and the Unchanging Real. This became her new faith. Quietly within herself she said something like this:

> I know that my body is spiritual substance. Since it is the substance of Spirit, nothing can fasten to it which could not fasten itself onto pure Spirit. Spirit could not be the subject of any destructive action; therefore nothing destructive can operate in me. Infinite perfection of Infinite Spirit is now working unhindered in every cell of my body, for I am consciously surrendered to its perfect working.

She was healed. She had discovered the healing power of a constructive faith. It was faith in the fact that her outer physical organism was merely the extension of Spirit in form, and that she as a thinker was the extension of Spirit creating new cells in the physical. She had learned that millions of new cells are being built in the body every minute, and she was determined to stamp each new cell with the image of perfection. Her demonstration of true faith, in thinking it, knowing it, living it, giving herself unreservedly to it, was like that of Naaman the Syrian who went down into the Jordan seven times until he came back with his flesh as pure as that of a little child.

It is a principle of Bible interpretation that water always refers to consciousness. The number seven always refers to perfection. One goes deep down into his consciousness. At first that consciousness may be quite imperfect, but he goes down again and again. Many of us have four or five or six sevenths of consciousness. Fear and other negative emotions are still mixed with our struggling faith.

We need to "be not weary in well doing, for in due season we shall reap if we faint not." We need to try for the highest, most perfect state of faith we can, for faith is the healing channel along which Omnipotence moves. That state arrives when we lose ourselves in the idea that there is an unchanging Reality that has never been marred, and when we lose ourselves in the serene tranquility of the Infinite, having abandoned ourselves to its perfect working.

Some persons say, "I agree intellectually with all that you say, but I have no faith. I hear of these things and know that they take place, but I don't seem to have the faith to bring them to myself. What can I do to get faith?"

EVERYONE HAS FAITH

The fact is that everyone has faith already. We do not acquire it. The capacity for faith is born with us. We do not originate it, nor do we whip it up by any mysterious formula. As one has said, "This great potential of faith is channeled through us; as we yield to it, it begins to operate." In our skins, we have the mechanisms for trapping sunlight and converting it into vitamin D; but we do not originate the vitamin; we merely convert it. In the same way, man has the ability to convert his thoughts into this life-giving vitamin of faith.

Faith and feeling are not the same thing. Many people stumble because they confuse the two. They are timorous; so they think they have no faith. Many persons have planted seeds for the first time. After poking their finger into the soil and dropping the seed they have thought, "These will not grow. I've never made anything grow in my lifetime. I just have the feeling they won't grow." But ten or fifteen days later the little green shoots were coming up.

They actually had faith in spite of their feelings. Their feelings said the seeds would not grow. Their faith was proved when they dropped in the seeds.

Faith is that which leads one into a definite course of action. It is fine if it is bolstered by a warm glow of feeling, but it is not dependent upon it in the slightest. Our feelings are often liars; they have to do with the senses. They are of the outside, less real world.

He who attends church instead of reading the Sunday paper at home has faith, proved by his works, even though he declares he doesn't believe a word that is said. Somewhere within him is an unrecognized faith that he will derive some particular benefit through his going to church. This is especially true of those who attend those churches which stress the healing power of faith, or read this book. They have faith already or they would not be reading it.

EXPAND THE AREA OF FAITH

When the individual can expand the area of his faith by reading or thinking upon the limitless marvels of the universe and of the Intelligence that brought it into being, he has gone a step further. He has taken his eyes off his faith or lack of it, and has centered his thought upon that which is the foundation of faith.

We may illustrate the previous paragraph by relating how Dr. Hubble brought a group of scientists down to the unveiling of the giant telescope in 1939. He showed them photographs of various universes extending limitlessly into space. Here were embryo universes; over there were adolescent universes; on this side were universes which had already arrived at maturity. Just as though he were demonstrating photographs of a human embryo developing through its various stages into birth, he explained that one single organizational plan ran through all of them.

We know that our sun and its planets are part of the galaxy known as the Milky Way, in which are a hundred million suns, so great as to dwarf our sun into nothingness. Light from far out in space travels at a speed of six trillion miles a year. This distance has become the astronomical unit for measuring distances in space. The "light year" is the yardstick of space. Yet some of the nebulae which Dr. Hubble had photographed were five hundred million "light years" distant.

Our faith becomes based upon something substantial when we come to know the immensity and vastness of the universe, and the even greater resources and power of the Intelligence that controls it.

Behind every sun and planet is the vast superintending Intelligence that directs their courses through space, always on time to the split second in their majestic march.

As one realizes what this implies concerning the marvelous infinitude of the Intelligence, his faith grows, for he comprehends that this same Intelligence controls the beat of our hearts. He is brought to the realization that, far off in space yet intimately within us, the one single organizational plan of which Dr. Hubble spoke is merely the outworking of an Infinite plan. In the field of inert matter, it conceives universes, develops them through their embryonic, adolescent, and mature stages. In the human field it produces spiritual beings through the same process.

INFINITE MIND IS INTERESTED IN US

Whether we have known it or not, the Infinite Mind evidently has enough interest in us to have built us and set us running. It has operated through us since conception, even though we have ignored or failed to see its co-operation. Then how much more we should expect it to heal us when we admit our past blindness and turn toward it, willing to co-operate with it. We may be sure of one thing: our faith based upon that knowledge can heal us.

Faith is not just a tickling of the imagination. Faith is an actual force—part of that force which swings giant suns in their courses—for faith is merely seeing things as God does, without fear or distortion. This enables Infinite Spirit to flow along the unobstructed channel of man's thought, no longer blocked by man's destructive fear patterns. Man's thought is magnified ten million times, invested as it is with that of the Infinite.

"NOT BY MIGHT NOR BY POWER . . ."

People sometimes wonder why we stress the ancient saying, "Not by might nor by power, but by my Spirit, saith the Lord." We do it because little man gets himself tensed and excited trying to *do* things. The more he fights and struggles, the more he obstructs that which never has to force or struggle. The secret of healing lies in "being," more than in "doing." He must learn to let himself go and to collaborate with that to which all things are possible.

Spirit is whatever Intelligence guides the heavenly bodies and superintends the building of an eight-pound baby from a fertilized ovum. Spirit lies at the center of the person, moving out through the mind and spiritualizing the understanding, then moving further out and spiritualizing the body in the mind's eye. Then that body becomes in actual experience that which Spirit always is in the innermost center—perfect and whole, lacking nothing.

Each day we should spend some time releasing ourselves to that healing Intelligence that indwells us. We should endeavor to forget ourselves, our struggles, efforts, weaknesses. We should turn away from past things of which we are ashamed and from places at which we have fallen short of our best. We should seek to lose ourselves in that sure, certain, orderly, adequate, resourceful fullness which characterizes the

Infinite Mind. Drawing away from whatever we have been in the past, we release ourselves daily to a new field of thought.

We begin to think as Spirit thinks. If there has been an enemy, we forgive him. If someone has hurt us, we stop brooding over it. If life has shaken us to our foundations, we say that life is friendly because the Infinite is friendly.

We rest then in the inner assurance of perfect law. We know that truth is truth even to the farthest star. Glimpsing what truth is, we yield ourselves to its operation in us. In clearing our own thought and uprooting all harsh feelings, we feel that we have done what is necessary. We release ourselves to that healing principle which was always ready and willing to heal, but which our distorted thought-patterns had shut out of our lives. Recognizing that the healing law will always operate at the highest level, we allow it to do so, and we rest ourselves in the quiet ceaseless movement of Infinite Mind, knowing that our changed thought is carried forward into its perfect manifestation.

Thus we prove the healing power of faith.

Chapter V

THE HEALING POWER OF A QUIET MIND

THE GREATEST need of the entire world today is for a quiet mind. In every stratum of society, in every town and village, the individual hungers for serenity and peace. Each war is entered upon with the promise that it will bring ultimate peace. But it proves to be only the prelude to another war.

Throughout the ages man has attempted to produce peace by the exterior methods of force. He has failed because true peace must always arise from a genuine spirit of good will within. They who would attempt to put it on like a coat of whitewash show that they misunderstand its nature.

The individual who would find peace in this changing world must likewise learn that it is neither given nor taken away by things external. True peace is always a state of mind originating within himself, based upon his choice of ancestry.

Man has a double ancestry. He inherits his animal, physical nature from his physical ancestors. He finds himself in possession of certain strengths and weaknesses, balances and imbalances, traits, characteristics, and tendencies. He soon learns that this physical nature is in conflict with a higher nature, which he has inherited from some Spiritual Source. His spiritual nature traces back in an unbroken line to eternity, and will endure long after he has left the earth scene.

He finds himself temporarily in possession of a physical body, which must be fed, clothed, and sheltered; therefore, it is natural that his principal efforts have been devoted to material acquisition. It is unfortunate that in his quest for these good things he has elevated them too often to the supreme place until today almost everything he prizes is measured in terms of money.

THE IMPONDERABLES

Man has missed the value of what some have called "the imponderables." He has failed to see that the greatest values lie hidden *within* the human race. Those which appear along the surface, while important to us as physical organisms living on a physical planet, are by no means as enduringly important as those intangibles hidden within.

It is possible to teach a class of businessmen certain business principles which will show up in the balance sheet in actual dollars and cents. But when we teach spiritual principles, it is not always so easy to classify and measure them. They are somewhat akin to that item on a firm's balance sheet listed as "good will," and which is sometimes set down at a million dollars among the assets, but which does not carry any substance apart from the business.

Where man has neglected the imponderables, he has never created a good society. Without them, our educational systems and churches would be worthless; indeed, our economic and political systems, even civilization itself, would be without value.

So long as man tries to patch up the world's ills without drawing upon the intensely potent spiritual forces of mankind, he is only spreading mild ointment upon a cancer. His best efforts are just as superficial as that.

This is why a cynic recently remarked that if a young person wished work which would guarantee him a lifetime job, he should fasten himself onto one of these peace societies which are working on the exterior aspects of man's conditions, ignoring the spiritual side. Then he will have a lifetime job, for he will never be able to bring peace to the world so long as the heart of man as an individual is left unchanged.

MAN IS THREE SIDED

In order to have a balanced view of life, we must recognize that man is three sided. Each side has its normal place and must be given due recognition.

His physical side drives him to set up a satisfactory industrial, economic, and political system. These should be the best he can construct. His mental side calls for an adequate educational system, which again should be the very best. His spiritual side calls just as loudly for the appeasement of his spiritual hungers.

This the churches have tried to furnish, but too often they have lost sight of their chief function, to "feed my sheep," and have become rigid systems of belief or ritual with little power to change men's lives at the center, or they have gone to the opposite extreme, stressing "social service" which occupies itself with the ointment when they should be getting at the bloodstream.

It has been amply demonstrated that the improvement of external conditions does not bring peace, for as long as man hungers spiritually, his mind can not become quiet. Some of those who live in luxury have the least inward peace. Man's three sides must balance if he is to enjoy serenity.

THE SPIRITUAL ASPECT

Some persons have a fairly well-balanced physical and mental life, yet are dead to the rich, warm spiritual experience. By the latter, we refer to that spiritual intuition which the mystics of the past and present have had. Whenever we use the term "mystic," we qualify it by explaining that we are not referring to a weird individual of eerie, mysterious mien consorting with spirits, or mixing up concoctions of the devil's brew, holding imaginary conversations with imaginary entities, letting his whiskers grow and going barefoot. This completely otherworldly creature is as unbalanced as the grossly animalistic.

The true mystic has set life over against itself. He knows the fleeting transitoriness of his physical segment in contrast to the eternal, enduring qualities of the spirit. He knows the value of the imponderables. He feels that in some way he is part of something larger than himself.

In the silence of his own mind, he allows the wheels of life to run slower, he drops the burdens and anxieties of the day in what has been called the secret place of the Most High.

And he emerges refreshed, with clearer mind and steadier purpose, because of this indefinable contact with Reality. In his withdrawn moments, he is made vividly aware of the essential oneness of the universe.

He senses that all life is one, and he is one with all life. He does not need to have the brotherhood of man preached to him, for he knows and feels it already. In fact he *is* it! He sees the gentleness under the apparent harshness of nature, the fairness beneath the apparent inequalities of life. He is no complainer.

We are impressed with the beauty of all things in the stillness of a mountain top, in an art gallery or a flower garden, perhaps in the presence of an infant. This unconscious recognition is in reality a mystical experience, for it is something apart from reasoning.

THE WISDOM OF THE AGES—THE CHRISTOS

The beauty which lies beneath the surface of things has been known since man became a thinker and observer. The deep, ageless Wisdom referred to in a previous chapter, haunting the bee, the flower, the atoms of the rock, the ancients called the *christos,* meaning the Wisdom, the Christ of the timeless ages. Long before Jesus was born, the Egyptians, Persians, Babylonians, and the people of India recognized this eternal Christ principle which is the sole possession of no one religion, since it is the basis for every true religion. The Christ is much more ancient than Christianity.

It is that which ceaselessly moves beneath the currents of life. Whenever man has contacted it, his body has been healed. It has lifted him from despondency to the heights, from defeat into triumph. It has untangled the perplexities of time because it is timeless. It molds and changes material form because it is above form. Far from being a person, it is the eternal Wisdom, timeless, ageless, undefeatable. It has nothing to do with theology. What a pity that the theologians have narrowed the concept to the one Man who allowed it to flow at full tide!

As a chip sometimes escapes from the rushing river crest and finds itself slowly circling in a quiet, eddying pool, so man, carried breathlessly on the turbulent currents of modern life, hungers for the quiet pools of the spirit. This is why a spiritual Sunday service allows him to step aside from the pull of external pressures, into a sphere where time is not important, into a state of consciousness in which he allows himself to become one with the *christos*.

The *christos* of the ages was never meant to be exclusively identified with any one man. Every reference to it denotes its impersonality. It is spoken of as Wisdom, the Logos or Word, the Way, Truth, Life, Vine. It is spoken of as the Door into man's larger life; whenever he wants to escape the turmoil of life he can do it only by stepping through that door and closing it after him, for then he is in the inner sanctuary of his own true being. The Bible calls it the

Light of Life, River of Life, Bread of Life, the Resurrection and the Life. It is always the impersonal Eternal Wisdom.

MAN'S EFFORT TO CONTACT THE WISDOM

Properly read, the Bible is the story of man's constant effort to contact that Wisdom which progressively expresses through man. Every higher ideal and spiritual aspiration man has ever had have been the faint whispers of this Wisdom as it moves forward in timeless progress.

Yielding himself to it, letting it work in and through him, man finds himself being carried without struggle toward his goal, be that goal health, happiness, or peace of mind. He does not produce his healing of himself. He becomes part of a flowing river wherein lie all the answers, and this oneness carries him forward in the onward cycle of fulfillment.

The Bible tells the story of paradise lost and paradise regained. The first and last books show this. This is important because unless it is read in this light the remainder of the Bible becomes meaningless and contradictory.

In Genesis, the earth was without form, and void; in Revelation, the city foursquare is clearly defined. In Genesis, darkness was upon the face of the earth;

in Revelation, there is no more night and they need not the light of the sun. In Genesis, all was chaotic; in Revelation, everything is in perfect order. In Genesis, we find the first sob and tear; in Revelation, God has washed away all tears. In Genesis, sin entered the world; in Revelation, sin is blotted out of remembrance. Genesis introduced illness; Revelation brings healing. Genesis brought in sorrow and gloom; Revelation portrays man as singing praises forever.

The Bible is not primarily a story in time; it is a story in consciousness. It depicts man's struggle to balance the physical with the spiritual. It is a psychological rather than a historical document, a saga of the protracted conflict between man's higher and lower natures. Man's human ancestry places him in Genesis; his spiritual ancestry brings him into the book of Revelation. Man can move from the chaos, tears, sins, illness, and darkness of Genesis into the order, joy, victory, health, and illumination of Revelation.

But it all must take place within himself. He must pass individually through the Door of the *christos* Wisdom into the place of the quiet mind. He must see himself as a branch of that eternal Vine, whose life flowing through him enables him to regain paradise.

We pointed out in a previous chapter that man thinks not alone with his brain but with every cell of his body. When he makes his way back into paradise, his mind settles down into tranquility, the arteries relax, the blood pressure returns to normal, digestion improves, the blood balances its white and red cells, the glands create their hormones, and the entire body chemistry is stabilized. Man thus experiences the healing power of the quiet mind, by knowing that Infinite Wisdom is not outside of him, but within him. "Lo, I am with you always" is the message of the *christos* spoken through the mouth of Jesus.

THE PROBLEMS OF EVIL AND SUFFERING

Two puzzling problems have always confronted man: the problem of evil on one hand, of suffering on the other. These never allow his mind to become quiet. As long as evil remains something separate, wished upon him against his will by someone outside himself, he remains unsettled. When he sees that his own thought is the arbiter of his destiny, he comes to understand that there is no problem of evil, for it is always being done unto him as he believes, and the kinds of thoughts he entertains determine that which shall be drawn into his life through the unfailing Law of Attraction, since like attracts like.

Shakespeare said that the fault lies not in our

stars but in ourselves that we are underlings. Eternal Truth says the same. We are not playthings of fate or of a cruel providence. We are magnets, and we must learn to be demagnetized to our lower ancestry and magnetized to the higher. Then just as impersonally shall we draw to ourselves all the riches of *christos.*

"Why does this happen to *me?*" "Why does so-and-so get all the breaks?" He who understands the truth of the *christos* never asks these questions. This strikes self-pity out of his life, which is one big advance in living, for self-pity is a wrecker of the quiet mind. Instead, he asks, "What in my thinking has attracted this to me?" and "What can I learn from this unhappy experience?" He knows that the universe is balanced and fair; so he withdraws to the center of life; again he begins deliberately to choose those threads of thought which will eventually be woven out into the stuff of life. The problems of evil and suffering are no longer problems because he sees life whole, and knows the Law of Cause and Effect.

THE GENTLENESS OF THE CHRISTOS

Modern psychology teaches the impersonal effects of what one thinks, but stops there. It lacks the deeper probing into the secret of the eternal *christos*, revealing the gentleness of the Infinite.

Hidden away in the stern ascetic utterances of the Old Testament is a sparkling diamond discovered by the ancient mystic who wrote it. He said, "Thy gentleness hath made me great." This inflexible old seer had passed under the discipline, whiplash, and anger of what he had thought to be God's punishment, and had been unchanged by it. But he now caught a glimpse of something tender, perhaps yearning, something which brought him to the point of gentleness with other sinners. He felt its influence within him, and he whispered contritely, "Thy gentleness hath made me great."

The *christos* never bullies nor forces its way with us. Its action is gentle, effortless, easy. It leads rather than drives.

Yet it is accompanied by actual force, more real and greater than electric power or steam. If it were not actual force, it could not alter morbid tissue into healthy cells; it could not draw actual customers to a salesman, nor open doors long closed against progress. All the theoretic academic teaching concerning it could not move one grain of sand unless there was an actual power accompanying it. It is as definite and specific in its action as an electric current at the turn of a switch when one learns how to speak his word for its movement into action.

Man ultimately arrives at the point where he sees that there has never been any malign influence teasing or blocking him, withholding his good from him. Illness and suffering have never been wished upon him without his consent. They have been attracted to him through his ignorance of the *christos*. Every blessing he desires is waiting for him. With the assurance that there is a Power ready to bring the good into his experience, he comes into a new-found quietness of mind. He is now linked to irresistible force.

THE POWER OF THE CHRISTOS

People think of disease in terms of curability or incurability; or they think a certain condition ought to take a week or a month to heal. For example, a person catches cold. He dabs away at it and thinks, "Oh well, it will be gone in a week when it runs its course." But within the scope of the *christos* Power that course could run in an hour or a minute. Instantaneous healing is merely the compressing of a time lapse into a shorter one. Perhaps we should say it is exchanging time for consciousness.

By surface massage and warmth, a limb may be restored in a few months. When that same limb is healed through spiritual treatment, it is the same process compressed in time. When Jesus healed the paralyzed man, time was compressed into a second.

From our human ancestry we have been bound by the concept of time. When we move over into the timeless *christos* we shall cease to block our healing by thinking that a certain time is required. Every cell of the body knows how to repair or renew itself. Our limited consciousness hinders them from doing it instantly. Let us develop the constantly expanding consciousness that this moment is all time compressed into a moment. Let us know that there are both willingness and power to heal.

We take the stretched-out concertina of time and press it gently but firmly together:

> Now, at this moment, in my body (or that of the person for whom I am treating), there is an instant *christos* Power, the Logos, Word, Door, River of Life, the Way, Truth and the Life, the Infinite Healing Presence. The *christos* in me now replaces everything that is unlike its own perfection, and I am healed.

Out of the *christos* comes the power, and out of the power comes the quiet mind; out of the quiet mind come the balanced emotions, and out of the balanced emotions comes the healing.

Other Books
by Frederick Bailes

HIDDEN POWER FOR HUMAN PROBLEMS

YOUR MIND CAN HEAL YOU

BASIC PRINCIPLES OF THE SCIENCE OF MIND
The Complete 12-Lesson Home-Study Course

COLLECTED ESSAYS OF FREDERICK BAILES

Healing the Incurable
Getting What You Go After
Is There a Cure for Frustration
Your Emotions Can Kill or Cure
The Secret of Healing
How to Get Along With Troublesome People
Help Answer Your Own Prayers

For more information, please write to:

DeVorss Publications
P.O. Box 550
Marina del Rey, CA 90294-0550